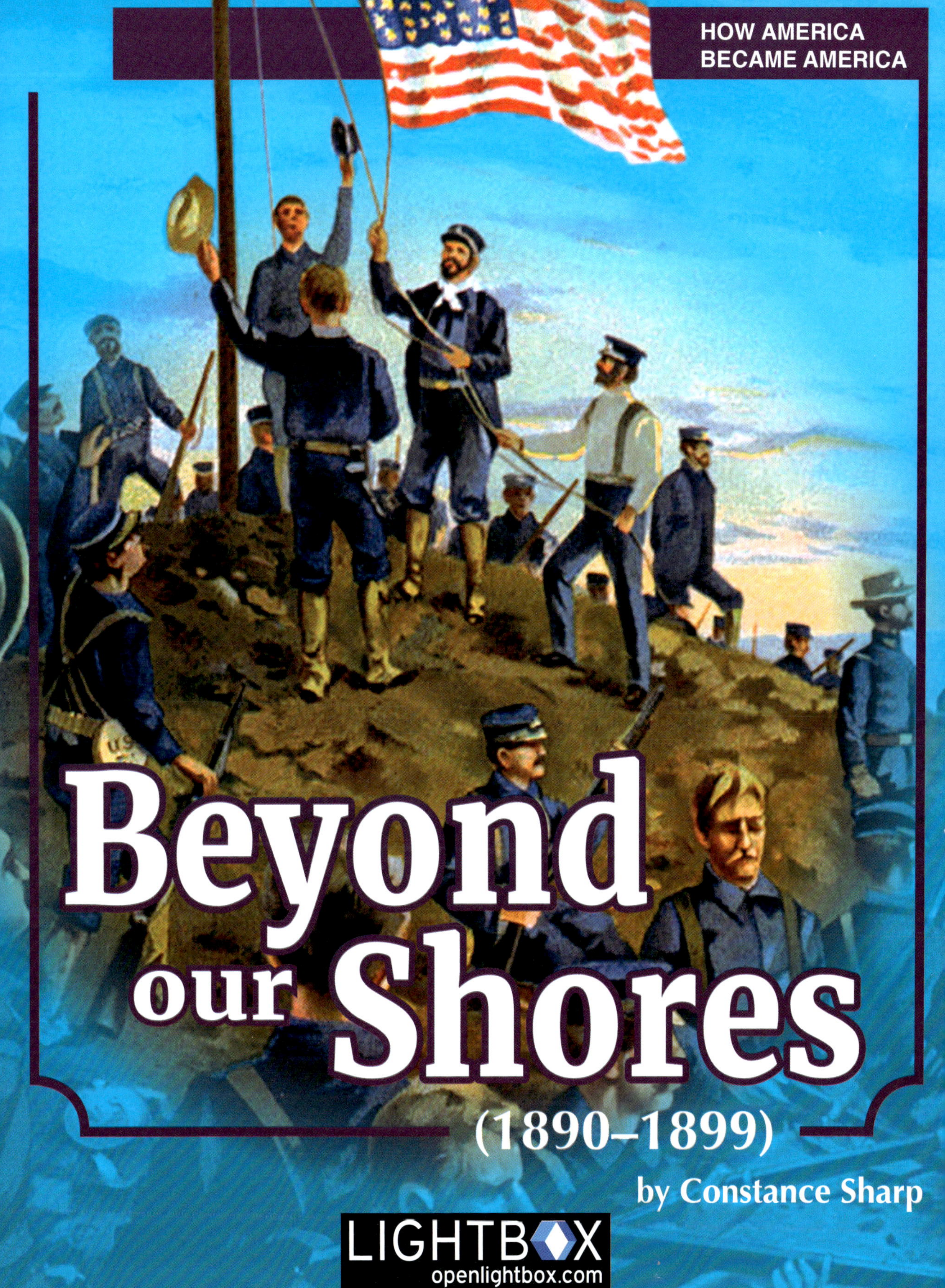
HOW AMERICA
BECAME AMERICA
Beyond
our Shores
(1890–1899)
by Constance Sharp
LIGHTBOX
openlightbox.com

Lightbox is an all-inclusive digital solution for the teaching and learning of curriculum topics in an original, groundbreaking way. Lightbox is based on National Curriculum Standards.

STANDARD FEATURES OF LIGHTBOX

AUDIO High-quality narration using text-to-speech system

ACTIVITIES Printable PDFs that can be emailed and graded

SLIDESHOWS Pictorial overviews of key concepts

VIDEOS Embedded high-definition video clips

WEBLINKS Curated links to external, child-safe resources

TRANSPARENCIES Step-by-step layering of maps, diagrams, charts, and timelines

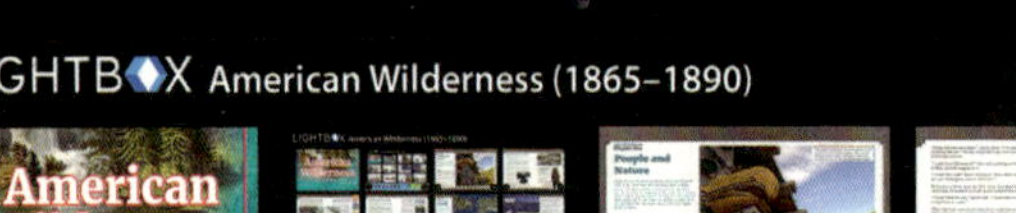

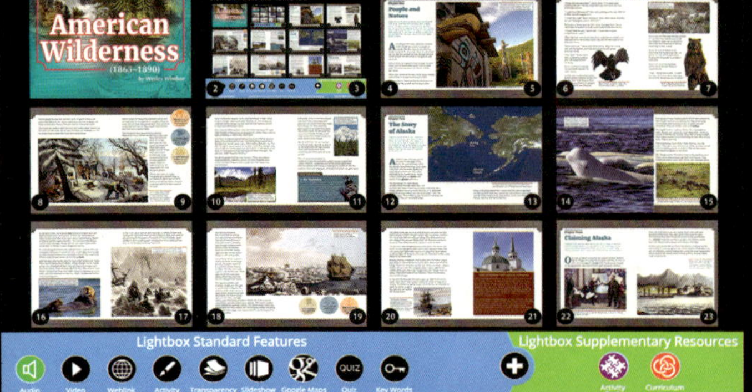

INTERACTIVE MAPS Interactive maps and aerial satellite imagery

QUIZZES Ten multiple choice questions that are automatically graded and emailed for teacher assessment

KEY WORDS Matching key concepts to their definitions

Contents

Chapter One

America Grows Up

Sooner or later, most children rebel against their parents. They want to stand on their own two feet. They no longer want to do everything their parents tell them to do. That's just part of growing up. And the young country of America felt the same way. America wanted to break away from her mother country, Great Britain.

Of course, the first time America rebelled was back in the 1700s. Americans fought the Revolutionary War so their country could be free from Great Britain, which is often called only Britain. But that was just the beginning. In some ways, America stayed close to Britain. After all, the two countries were a lot alike. Many Americans came from Britain. They still had friends and family in Britain. In many ways, Americans and the British still thought the same way. They had the same values. Many of the same things were important to them.

Meeting in 1776, American leaders approved the Declaration of Independence, stating their reasons for wanting to separate from Great Britain.

Beginning in 1837, Queen Victoria ruled Britain for 64 years. During that time, Britain gained control of many areas around the world.

But in other ways, Britain and America were very different. Sometimes, America wanted one thing, while Britain wanted something else. Just like in any family, they had arguments. They bumped heads.

And at the same time, both countries were changing. They were both getting bigger. By the late 1800s, America was no longer a baby nation. And Britain had turned into an **empire**.

"The sun never sets on the British Empire" was a common saying in those days. That meant that the British Empire stretched all the way around the globe. At any hour, somewhere, the sun was shining on British land.

As children grow up, they often imitate their parents. That's what the United States did. By the end of the 19th century, America was trying to break away further from Britain. At the same time, America was trying to be more like Britain. Americans were thinking about building their own empire.

James Monroe was president of the United States from 1817 to 1825.

Back in the early 1800s, President James Monroe made an important statement. His statement is called the Monroe Doctrine. That statement would shape the way America thought of itself all the way up to the 21st century.

The Monroe Doctrine said that European nations could no longer build **colonies** in North America or South America. Then, it went one step further. It said that it was the United States' job to protect North and South America from other countries. This meant America had the right to get mixed up in any war that took place in North or South America. This happened in 1895.

Great Britain had a colony in Guiana, on the continent of South America. The land lay along the border of Venezuela. Venezuelans said that Britain had claimed several hundred miles of their land. Venezuela wanted the countries of the world to help it settle the question. Britain refused to even talk about it. The two countries had been angry with each other for years.

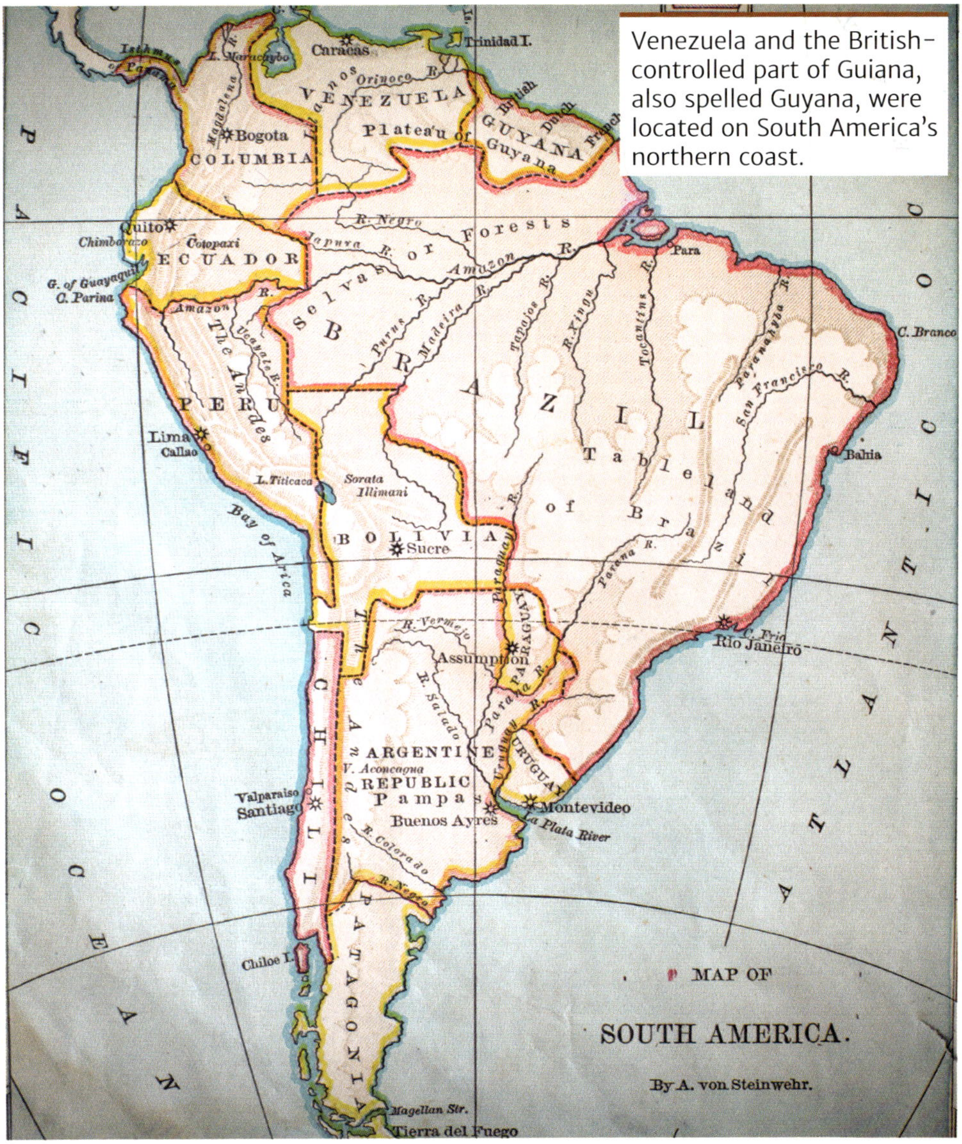

Venezuela and the British-controlled part of Guiana, also spelled Guyana, were located on South America's northern coast.

President Monroe stated the **Monroe Doctrine** in a message to Congress in **1823**.

By **1901**, the British Empire included **one-fifth** of the world's land.

President Ronald Reagan used the Monroe Doctrine in the **1980s** as a reason for U.S. fighting in **Central America**.

Grover Cleveland won the U.S. presidential election in 1892. He was worried that Britain might claim even more land in South America. He didn't want that to happen.

He didn't want Great Britain to become any stronger than it was already. So he wrote a letter to Great Britain.

The British were angry. They said that the Monroe Doctrine was just something Americans had made up. The British didn't think it was a real law.

Grover Cleveland was inaugurated, or sworn in, as president in early 1893 at a ceremony in Washington, D.C.

EMPIRES IN HISTORY

One of the earliest and most powerful empires was the Roman Empire. About 2,000 years ago, Roman soldiers conquered much of Europe, as well as parts of Asia and Africa. Centuries later, European powers such as Spain, Britain, and France built their own empires. They built colonies on the land that they took over on the other side of the Atlantic Ocean, as well as in Asia and Africa. Slowly, Spain and France became less powerful. Britain grew in strength. The British Empire remained powerful until the second half of the 20th century.

Now President Cleveland was angry. He didn't want a war. But he didn't want to back down either.

The British didn't want a war either. Eventually, they agreed to let an **international tribunal** settle their argument with Venezuela. The tribunal came up with a compromise. Great Britain would get to keep the land it had already claimed. It could not claim any more land, though.

Nothing much happened really. But it was important because this was the first time America had acted on the Monroe Doctrine. It was the first time the United States insisted it had the right to get mixed up in something that had nothing to do with America.

History is full of stories. The people who take part in events all have their own stories. Those stories depend on their point of view. For example, think about the stories the American settlers told. Those stories had to do with courage and freedom. Then, think of the stories told by Native American people who lost their lands to those settlers. Their stories would have been very different. Both sets of stories have their own truth.

The British did not want to give up land in South America on which they grew sugarcane. They made a great deal of money from selling sugarcane, which grows well in Guiana's warm climate.

Stories are also powerful. They help shape the future. They push people to act in certain ways. The Monroe Doctrine was one of those powerful stories.

The Monroe Doctrine would lead the United States into war. It would play a big role in many of America's stories for years to come. Those stories would end up touching the lives of countless people who lived in other lands. One of those lands was the peaceful island nation of Hawai'i.

GET THINKING

Good and Bad Features of Empires

Empires can be good in some ways for areas controlled by another country. The stronger country can bring schools, better roads, and better health care to these areas. In other ways, though, empires can be bad. They take away the freedom of people in controlled areas.

What do you think? Are empires good or bad?

Victoria Memorial Hall, an art museum, was built in Kolkata, India, in the early 1900s to honor Britain's Queen Victoria. India was part of the British Empire until 1947.

Chapter Two

Hawai'i

Long before America came to Hawai'i, the people who lived there had their own stories. The Hawai'ians said that Papa, the Earth-Mother, and Wakea, the Sky-Father, had given birth to the islands of Hawai'i and Maui. Their grandchild was the ***taro*** *plant. Everything was linked together. The world was alive. It breathed. It was like a person. It grew. It was good.*

Stories like these were passed down from parents to children for hundreds of years. They had been brought to Hawai'i hundreds of years ago by Polynesian settlers. These people used boats they designed and built to sail long distances. They explored the entire Pacific Ocean. They settled on the islands.

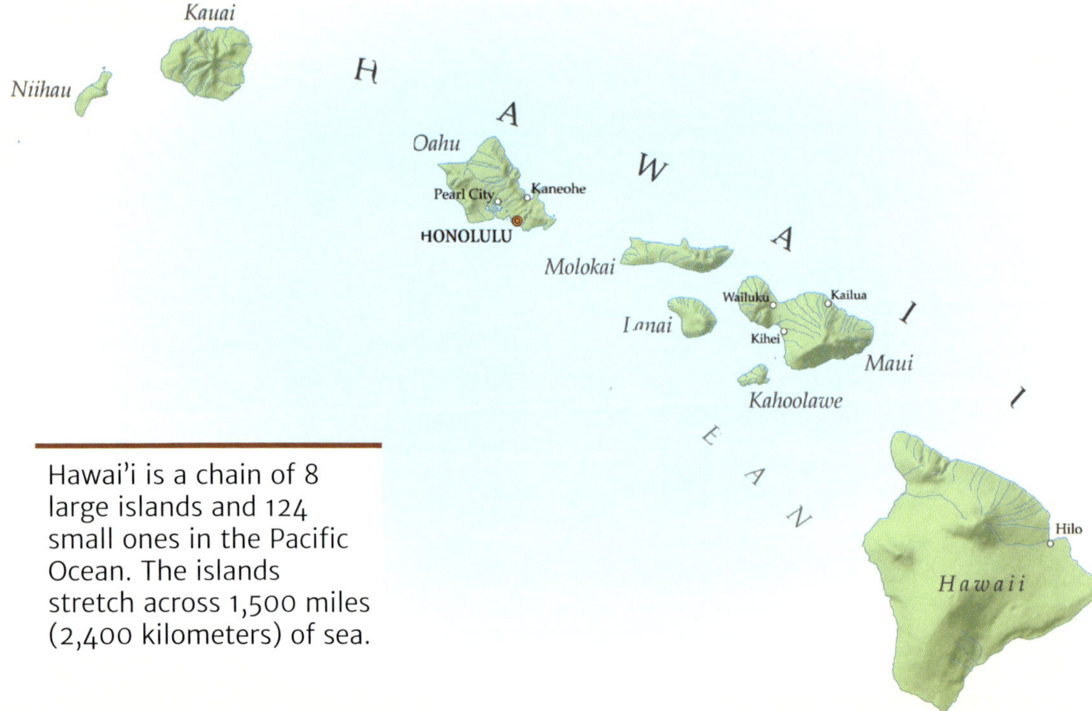

Hawai'i is a chain of 8 large islands and 124 small ones in the Pacific Ocean. The islands stretch across 1,500 miles (2,400 kilometers) of sea.

Ancient Polynesian Sailing Boat

Ancient Polynesians hollowed out a large tree to form the hull, or base, of the boat. A second hull, called an outrigger, kept the boat steady. The boom and mast held the sail steady and tight against the wind.

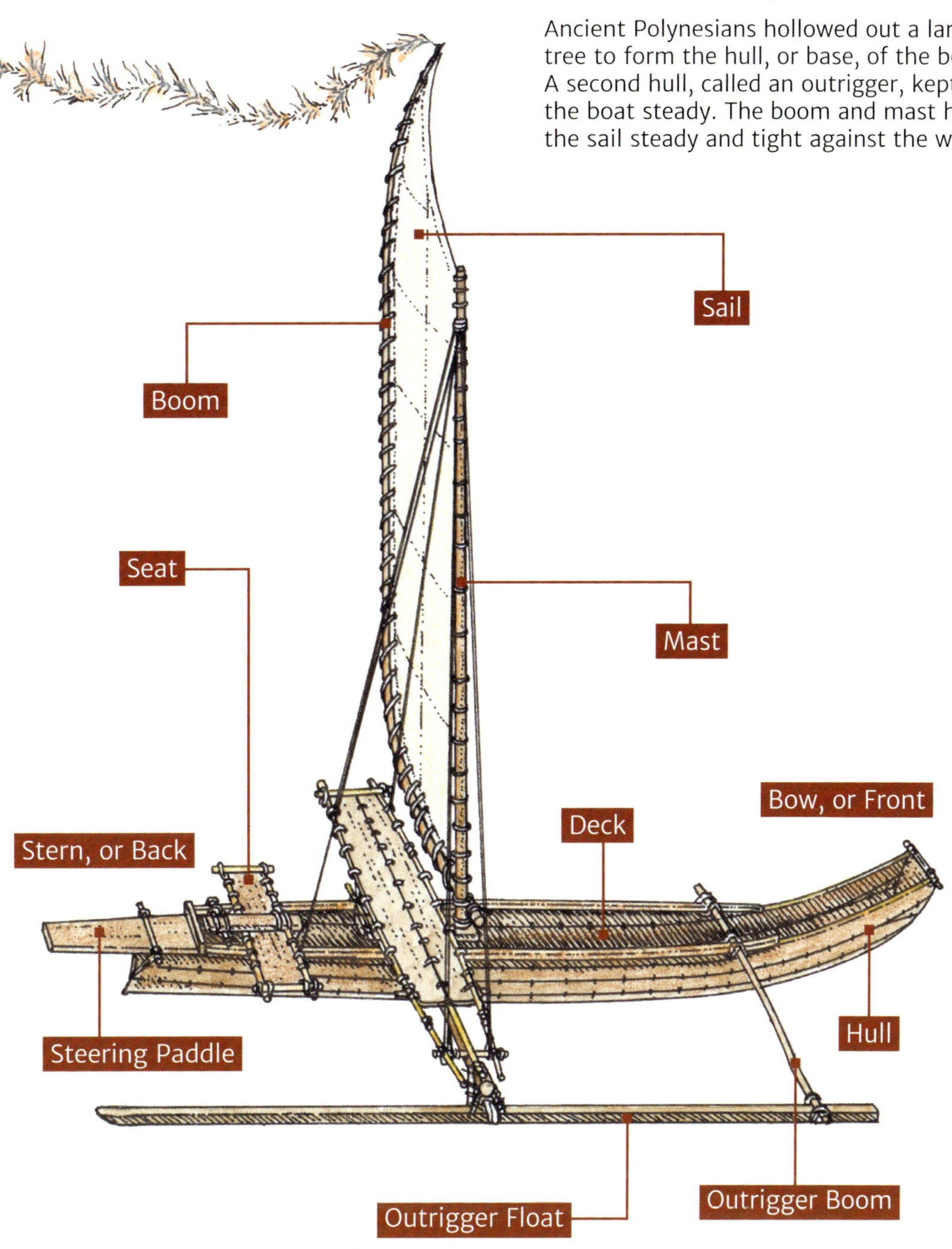

Centuries before Europeans ever dared to sail out into the Atlantic Ocean, the ancient Hawai'ians were sailing all over the Pacific. They understood the natural world in ways that Europeans didn't. This made them good sailors.

At home, they were also good farmers. They grew more than 200 kinds of sweet potatoes and taro. They used **irrigation** to water their fields. Their farming was so good that they didn't have to work very hard to feed lots of people.

Statues guarded the entrance to an ancient Hawai'ian temple.

POLYNESIA

In the South Pacific Ocean, there is a group of more than 1,000 small islands. These are known as Polynesia. The Native people who live in these islands share many of same customs and beliefs. They speak the same language. Hundreds of years ago, Polynesian sailors learned to use the stars for direction.

Most ancient Hawaiians only worked about four hours a day. But they built the largest temples in all the Pacific. They also built the fastest canoes. They created beautiful dances and poetry. They made cloth out of bark.

These people weren't perfect. They could be mean to each other. But most of the time, they lived in peace. They saw God everywhere. They prayed about everything. They had rules that told them how to get along with each other. They shared the land where they lived. They shared the work. They shared their food. And they hardly ever got sick. They'd never even had a cold!

In 1778, everything changed in Hawai'i. A British explorer named Captain James Cook landed on one of the Hawai'ian islands. Now, the rest of the world would find out about Hawai'i and its people. Their peaceful, ancient way of living would come to an end.

In the years to come, American and British ships often stopped at the Hawai'ian islands. The ships would stock up there on food and fresh water. The sailors told other people about how beautiful the islands were. Other white people started coming to the islands.

After Europeans and Americans reached Hawai'i, the settlement of Honolulu grew to become a major port.

The **first** Polynesians to reach Hawai'i probably traveled more than **2,300 miles** (3,760 km) from the Marquesas Islands.

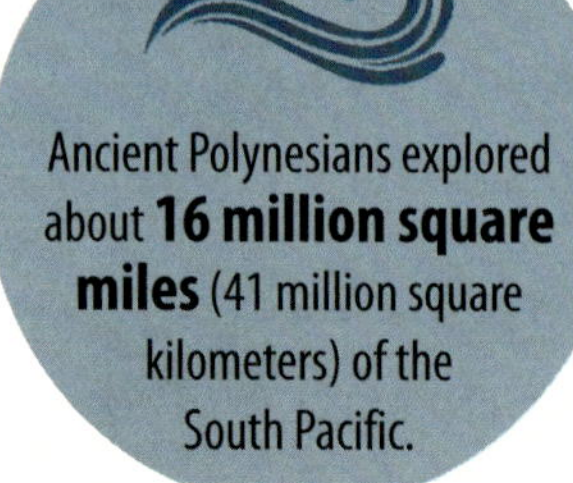

Ancient Polynesians explored about **16 million square miles** (41 million square kilometers) of the South Pacific.

At least **300,000** Native people were living in Hawai'i when Europeans arrived.

They brought change with them. They didn't follow the laws that Hawai'ians had followed for centuries. The Hawai'ians saw that nothing happened to the white people who broke the laws. Soon, some Hawai'ians no longer followed the ancient laws either. This meant that their whole way of life would begin to change.

The white people also brought germs with them. The people who lived on the islands had no **immunity** against these germs. Thousands and thousands of Hawai'ians got sick and died.

Missionaries also came to Hawai'i. They taught Christianity to the Hawai'ians. But they also taught the Hawai'ians about other things. White people didn't understand the islanders' religion. The Hawai'ians' way of living made no sense to them. They thought they were helping the Hawai'ians by teaching them new ways of doing things.

Mokuaikaua Church is the oldest Christian church on the Hawai'ian islands. It was built in 1837.

Hawai'ians had never used money. They didn't own land. Instead, they shared everything. Now, though, they learned about money. They learned about being rich. They learned to own land. Instead of growing crops to share with each other, now they learned to sell their crops for money. Instead, of growing food for themselves, they started growing sugarcane to sell.

In the decades after Captain Cook arrived in Hawai'i, everything changed. Before long, the Monroe Doctrine would also reach Hawai'i. And then everything would change even more.

James Drummond Dole moved to Hawai'i from Massachusetts in 1899. The next year, he bought land and started a pineapple **plantation**. In 1901, he founded the Hawaiian Pineapple Company. The company planted and grew pineapples. Then, it picked the pineapples and put them in cans. It shipped the pineapples to America. For the first time, Americans could buy pineapple in almost any grocery store.

Dole was an honest businessman. He didn't understand that his business was helping to change Hawaiians' lives.

The company James Drummond Dole started still grows pineapples in Hawai'i today.

In the late 1800s, people from Britain were also building businesses in Hawai'i. Great Britain hoped that Hawai'i would become part of the British Empire. The United States didn't want that to happen. The Americans who lived in Hawai'i didn't want it to happen either. Using the Monroe Doctrine again, America told Great Britain to back off.

The Americans who lived in Hawai'i were less than 20 percent of the whole population. But they controlled more than 80 percent of the islands' wealth. This made them very powerful. They decided to form their own government.

Fields of pineapples made some Americans rich, but Native Hawai'ians who did not own farms could not make money from sales of pineapple crops.

In 1893, Americans took Hawai'i away from its queen. Sanford B. Dole, who was James Dole's older brother, became the president of the new government. The new government wrote new laws. Now, only people who owned large pieces of land could vote. People who could not read, write, or speak English could not be **citizens**. This left out most of the Native Hawai'ians.

The new government wanted Hawai'i to become part of the United States. The white landowners knew this was the best way to protect their land and businesses from the British.

In 1898, America went to war with Spain. Some of the fighting in the Spanish-American War took place in the Philippines, a group of islands in the western Pacific Ocean. Hawai'i was a good stopping place for U.S. warships headed to those islands. The United States realized that having a naval base at Hawai'i could be a good idea. Americans didn't want Spain to attack Hawai'i.

Ash from the Hawai'ian islands' volcanoes made land fertile, or good for growing crops. American farmers wanted this rich land.

In 1898, Hawai'i became part of the United States. Sanford Dole now became the governor of the new **territory**. His government continued to rule the islands for several years. Citizens of the new land were now citizens of the United States. At first, people who had not been citizens, including most Native Hawaiians, could not be American citizens.

The Monroe Doctrine was changing the entire world. Other islands in the Pacific Ocean were also being changed. As a result of the Spanish-American War, the Philippines became U.S. land. So did Guam, another Pacific island. Like Hawai'i, these islands also had their own stories to tell.

A SAD DAY FOR HAWAI'I

The Hawai'ian government had a big ceremony and party on August 12, 1898, the day when Hawai'i became a part of the United States. But the woman who had been queen, Queen Liliuokalani, did not go to the party. Many Native Hawaiians gathered at the Queen's home. For them, it was the saddest day they had ever known.

Today, many people in Hawai'i still feel that Hawai'i should be a separate free country. They want to give Hawai'i back to Native Hawai'ians. In 1993, the U.S. government did apologize to Native Hawai'ians for overthrowing their kingdom. For some Hawai'ians, this apology is too little too late.

U.S. Territories in the Pacific

CANADA

UNITED STATES

MEXICO

1 Guam

At least 3,000 years ago people from Indonesia and from the Philippines settled on the island of Guam. Spain officially claimed the island in 1564 and then gave it to the United States in 1898. Hagåtña is the capital.

2 American Samoa

American Samoa includes several islands. In 1878, the United States began building a U.S. Navy base there. American Samoa became an official U.S. territory in 1929. Pago Pago is the capital.

Spain controlled the Philippines for more than 300 years, until 1898. The islands became completely independent of the United States in 1946. Manila is the capital.

3 Philippines

4 Northern Mariana Islands

People from Southeast Asia were the first to settle on these 22 islands. Then, Spain ruled them, followed by Germany, Japan, and the United States. The area is now a U.S. **commonwealth**. Its capital is in Saipan.

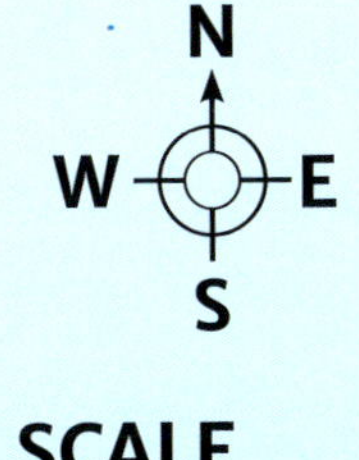

SCALE

0 — 1000 Miles
1609.34 Km

LEGEND

- Water
- Historical U.S. Territories
- Other Land
- ★ Capitals
- The Continental United States

Chapter Three

Cuba

More than 500 years ago, a man named Hatuey led a group of canoes to the island of Cuba in the Caribbean Sea. When he landed, he told a story to the islanders who lived there. His story made them tremble with fear.

Hatuey said white-skinned men had come to his land, the nearby island of Hispaniola. They had been dressed in shiny metal. They carried weapons harder than stone. They were cruel. They treated human beings worse than they treated animals. They had killed and hurt Hatuey's people. The only thing they cared about was gold.

Hatuey led a group of 400 people from Hispaniola to Cuba. Today, a statue honoring him stands in the Cuban city of Baracoa.

These white-skinned men would come to the island of Cuba, too, Hatuey warned. He wanted the islanders in Cuba to help him fight the strangers.

The islanders couldn't believe Hatuey's story. Only a few of them agreed to help him fight the light-skinned men.

CUBA IS CLOSE

Cuba is the largest island in a group of islands that makes up the modern-day country of Cuba. The island is about 90 miles (about 150 km) south of Florida. The nation of Cuba has an area of 42,800 square miles (110,860 sq. km). This makes it a little smaller than the state of Pennsylvania.

Christopher Columbus was an Italian explorer. He convinced the king and queen of Spain to pay for a voyage to find new **trade routes**. Columbus reached the Caribbean in October 1492. He explored the Bahamas and some other islands. Then he went home. He brought stories with him. These were powerful stories. They told about a land filled with gold and riches.

On his first trip to the Caribbean, Columbus landed on the island of San Salvador in the Bahamas. He claimed the area for Spain.

Columbus came back to the Caribbean region several times. He made a total of four voyages to the area by 1502. Many Spanish settlers followed.

The Spanish were disappointed that they didn't find more gold than they did on islands like Cuba. But the Spanish soon realized they could get rich from Cuba in other ways.

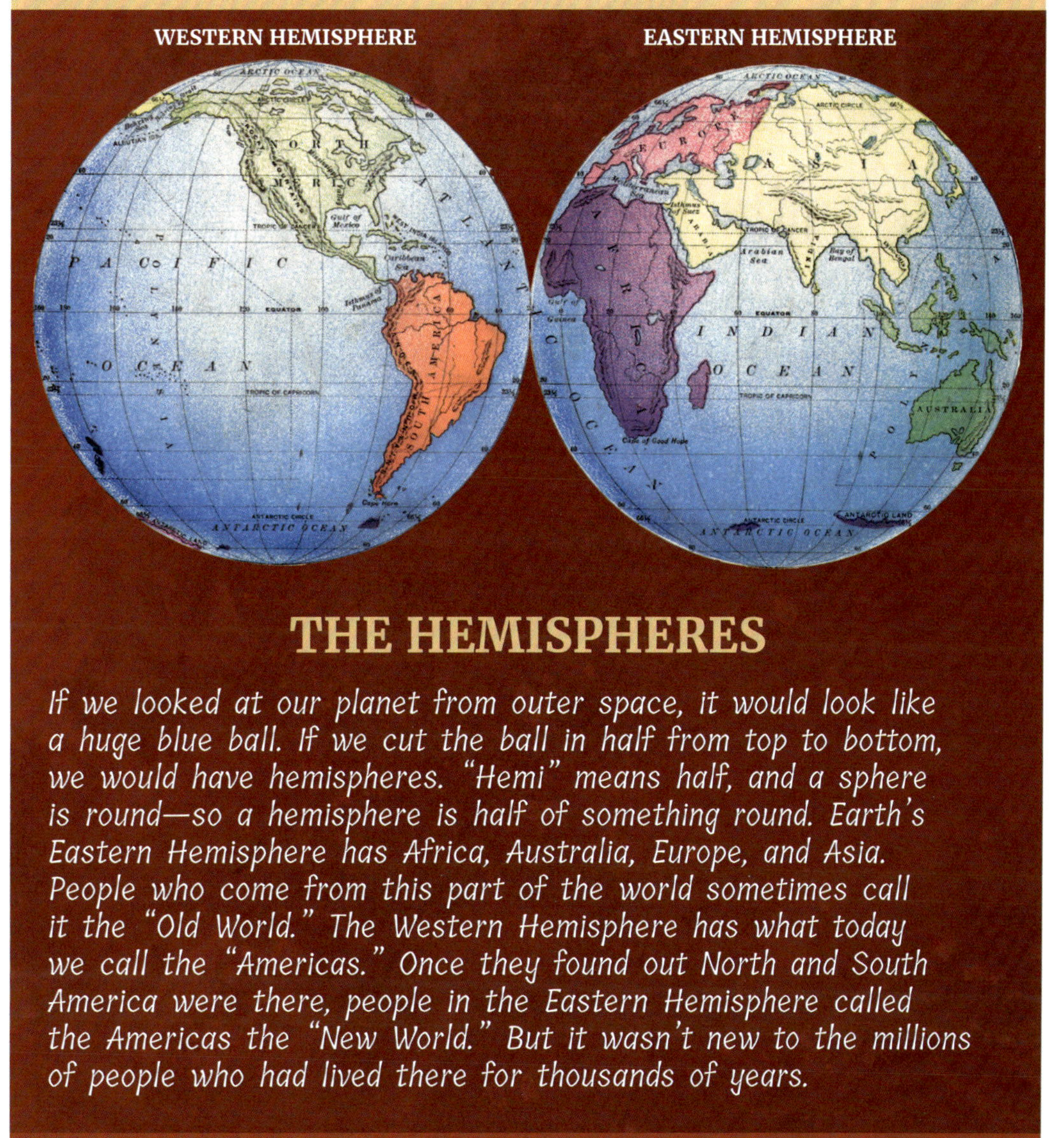

THE HEMISPHERES

If we looked at our planet from outer space, it would look like a huge blue ball. If we cut the ball in half from top to bottom, we would have hemispheres. "Hemi" means half, and a sphere is round—so a hemisphere is half of something round. Earth's Eastern Hemisphere has Africa, Australia, Europe, and Asia. People who come from this part of the world sometimes call it the "Old World." The Western Hemisphere has what today we call the "Americas." Once they found out North and South America were there, people in the Eastern Hemisphere called the Americas the "New World." But it wasn't new to the millions of people who had lived there for thousands of years.

CHRISTOPHER COLUMBUS AND THE ARAWAKS

In 1492, when Columbus landed in the Western Hemisphere, he believed he had traveled full circle around the world. He thought he had landed in the East Indies, a part of Asia. That's why he called the people he met "Indians." Really, however, he had landed in the Caribbean region.

Columbus and his men found peaceful Native people called the Arawaks. There were hundreds of thousands of them, maybe even millions. They gave food and friendship to the newcomers.

However, Spanish settlers made them into slaves. They killed them. Without meaning to, they also spread new germs to them. In just a few years after Columbus's first voyage, hundreds of thousands of Arawaks had died. Within 50 years, only a few hundred of them were left. In 150 years, every single Arawak was probably dead.

The island had good farmland. And it turned out that sugarcane grew well there. Sugarcane became Cuba's new "gold."

The Spanish built huge sugarcane plantations. These plantations needed lots of workers. After the Native people were all dead, the Spanish brought slaves to Cuba from Africa.

Some of Cuba's best farmland is found in the Viñales Valley.

A few hundred years after Columbus came to Cuba, the people who lived there were completely different. The Arawaks were all gone. Instead, Africans and Spaniards lived there. Some of the Africans and Spaniards had had children together—and then these children had had children of their own.

These groups of people wanted different things. Some of them wanted to be completely free from Spain. They wanted to be their own country.

Others wanted to stay a part of Spain. And still others wanted to become part of the United States. By the early 1890s, all these groups of people had been fighting against each other and against Spain for more than 20 years. They were worn out. Their country was poor.

But they didn't give up. In 1895, yet another rebellion began. Spain hit back. Hard. But the Cuban rebels didn't give up. People kept fighting for three more years. And now Americans were getting more interested.

The U.S. government kept a close eye on the revolution. There were American businesses in Cuba. Thousands of American citizens lived in Cuba. The United States wanted to protect these people and businesses.

The United States was also interested in making Cuba a state. It wanted Cuba for some of the same reasons that Spain had. Cuba had good land. It could make the United States a lot of money.

It wasn't until the mid-20th century that people discovered that the U.S.S. *Maine* had accidentally blown up.

For a while, the United States didn't do any fighting in Cuba. It did send some battleships to wait off the coast. One day, a ship named the U.S.S. *Maine* mysteriously exploded. No one knew why. But Americans were sure that Spain had done it.

The biggest sea battle of the Spanish-American War was fought in Manila Bay, near the Philippines. U.S. warships defeated a Spanish fleet, or group of ships.

The United States went to war against Spain. Suddenly, the Cuban revolution changed names. It was now the Spanish-American War.

Four months later, the fighting was over. Spain surrendered. But not to Cuban rebels. It surrendered to the United States.

Now, instead of Spain as their ruler, Cubans had the United States. Many Cubans had wanted complete freedom. They were free from Spain now. But they were worried about becoming part of the United States.

The American military was in Cuba. The United States took part in making Cuba's new government. It took over Cuban trade. It seemed like the United States was taking over Cuba.

A MAN WHO WOULD BE PRESIDENT

One of the soldiers who fought in the Spanish-American War was a man named Theodore Roosevelt. He led a group of soldiers known as the Rough Riders. Roosevelt and the Rough Riders fought in Cuba. They helped win the war. Many Americans thought of Roosevelt as a hero.

One day, he would become the president of the United States.

More than **300,000** American troops took part in the **Spanish-American War**.

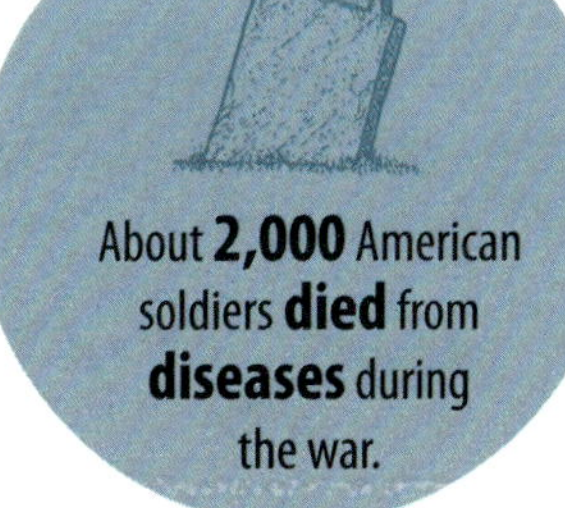

About **2,000** American soldiers **died** from **diseases** during the war.

Fewer than **400** U.S. troops **died** in **combat** against Spanish forces.

Chapter Four

Puerto Rico

Some Americans called the Spanish-American War "a splendid little war." They thought it had been an easy war to fight. And in the end, the United States ended up with more land. Cuba was now part of the United States. So were the Philippines. And so was another Caribbean island, Puerto Rico.

A long time ago, there were only a few people who lived on the island of Puerto Rico. These Natives were called the Arawaks. They were short. They had straight, black hair. They wore a lot of jewelry made out of shells, bones, clay, and gold. They didn't wear a lot of clothes.

Rainforests covered large parts of Puerto Rico when the Arawaks lived there.

WAR

Actually, no war is splendid! Many people were hurt and died in the Spanish-American War. In addition to the 2,400 American soldiers who died during the war, more than 1,600 U.S. troops were injured. Thousands of Spanish troops, as well as people in Cuba and the Philippines, also lost their lives.

They didn't call their island Puerto Rico. That's a Spanish name. These people didn't speak Spanish. Instead, they spoke their own language. In their language, the island was called Boriquen.

The Arawaks sometimes fought with another group of people, called the Caribs. They mostly lived in peace, though. That all changed when new people came from Spain.

A statue of Christopher Columbus now stands in San Juan, Puerto Rico's capital city.

The Arawaks looked pretty strange to Columbus and his crew when they first landed on Puerto Rico in 1493. The Arawaks had dark skin. They didn't wear many clothes. They spoke a different language. The Spanish looked pretty strange to the Arawaks, too. They had light skin and beards. They had huge wooden ships that rose high out of the water. The men had metal armor and weapons such as swords and pistols.

The Spanish renamed everything. They couldn't speak the native language so they named the island and its people in Spanish. They called the Arawaks "Tainos." They called the island's biggest city "Puerto Rico."

Columbus eventually left, but in 1508, a man named Ponce de León came back. He came back to build a fort. He also wanted to colonize the island. Ponce de León brought lots of people to live there. He brought farmers. He brought priests. He brought builders. He brought all the people he needed to make a Spanish town.

Ponce de León claimed the island for Spain. This meant Spain owned it. Ponce de León didn't care about the Arawaks. He didn't ask them if they wanted to give up their island. They had lived there a long time—but now, the Spanish took over.

Ponce de León built the settlement of Caparra in 1508. It was Puerto Rico's first capital city.

The Spanish started digging for gold. They wanted to get rich. That was why they wanted the island.

They also made the Arawaks into slaves. They wanted the Arawaks to be more like the Spanish. So they made them wear Spanish clothes. They made them worship God the way the Spanish did. They taught them the Spanish language.

San José Church, built beginning in 1532 in San Juan, is the oldest church in Puerto Rico.

Many African slaves were taken on ships to the Caribbean, where they were traded for molasses. This sweet syrup was made into rum in America. The rum was then traded for more slaves in Africa.

Some of the Arawaks tried to fight back. But the Spanish were too strong. They killed 6,000 Arawaks. By now, most of the Native people had disappeared. Some had died. Some had run away to live somewhere else. The island was Spanish.

The Spanish started farming the island. Puerto Rico had good land. It could grow good food. It could also grow sugarcane. Sugarcane is made into sugar. Sugar used to be very expensive. If you could grow and sell sugar, you would be rich.

Who would do the farming? All the Native slaves had either died or escaped. The Spanish wouldn't do the farming. They didn't want to

The Spanish built a fort called Castillo San Felipe del Morro to defend San Juan from attacks by pirates and by other countries.

do all the hard work. There weren't enough of them either. So they brought in more slaves. This time, they shipped slaves in from Africa. The Africans worked on the sugar farms.

It wasn't an easy life for anyone. People kept on dying of disease. Even the Spanish died. Pirates and Native groups often attacked the island.

People knew the Spanish were getting rich in Puerto Rico. The Spanish had found gold, silver, and pearls. Thieves attacked the Spanish so they could steal the treasure.

After a while, the treasure ran out. Even farming wasn't good. Puerto Rico became poor. The Spanish people didn't really want to live there anymore. Most of them moved away.

Spain kept forts on Puerto Rico to protect the land. Armies from other countries kept attacking the forts. These other countries wanted to own the islands in the Caribbean, including Puerto Rico.

The Spanish brought ginger to grow in Puerto Rico. The root of this plant is used as a spice.

Who lived on Puerto Rico now? There were two groups of people. One group was Spanish. They had moved to Puerto Rico straight from Spain. Or they were born in Puerto Rico but had two parents who were Spanish. The Spanish people living in Puerto Rico were rich. They owned big farms. They had slaves.

There was another group of people, too. They were called Creoles. When the Spanish first came to Puerto Rico, some of them married Natives. Later, Africans came to the island. Some Spanish people married them. The children of parents who came from two different types of people were called Creoles. A Creole person might have an African mother and a Spanish father. He or she could have a Native mother and an African father. Creole just meant that you weren't pure Spanish.

In the late 1800s, about 85 percent of Puerto Ricans lived in the countryside. Many of the homes were small huts.

Creoles were poor. They farmed tiny pieces of land. Many Spanish people thought Creoles were not as good as the Spanish.

Spain didn't treat Puerto Ricans very well. The governors of the island were cruel. They were especially cruel to Africans, Natives, and Creoles. Puerto Rico wanted to be free from Spain.

After the Spanish-American War, Puerto Rico belonged to the United States. Now, America controlled Puerto Rico. Puerto Ricans were glad to be free from Spain, but they weren't sure yet whether they wanted to be part of the United States.

By about 1900, bananas had become a popular fruit in the United States. Some U.S. businesses started banana plantations in Puerto Rico.

The United States gained **126,000 square miles** (326,000 sq. km) of territory at the end of the Spanish-American War.

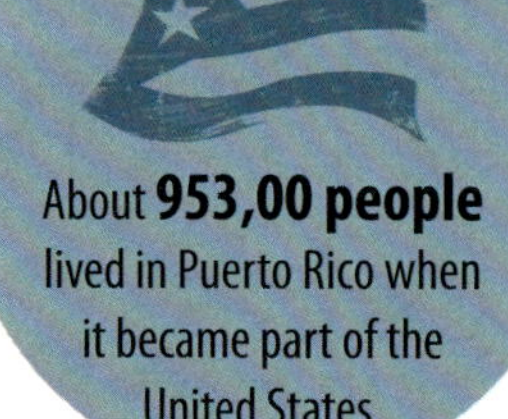

About **953,00 people** lived in Puerto Rico when it became part of the United States.

Today, Puerto Rico's population is **3.4 million**.

Now, America was building its own empire, just like Great Britain had. Americans were proud that their country was growing. Many Americans truly believed that other lands would be better off if they belonged to the United States. They believed that if the United States kept spreading, getting bigger and bigger, the world would be a better place.

And as the country entered the 20th century, it wasn't just growing larger. It was also growing more powerful. Soon it would be ready to take part in one of the biggest wars the world had ever known.

GET THINKING

True Stories?

Americans told themselves a story that said it would be good for people in other lands to belong to the United States. Do you think there were any other stories being told at the same time? What story do you think the people of Hawai'i told their children about the United States' takeover? What story did the people of Cuba, the Philippines, and Puerto Rico tell? Do you think there was more than one story to tell in each of these islands? Do you think just one story was true? Or could more than one story be true?

The United States insisted to countries in the Caribbean that they would be better off with U.S. help than with European aid.

Timeline

1778—James Cook lands on one of the Hawai'ian islands.

1493—Christopher Columbus lands in Puerto Rico.

1500

1600

1700

1800

1511—Hatuey flees the island of Hispaniola for Cuba.

1519—European explorer Ferdinand Magellan, sailing for Spain, arrives in the Philippines, where he loses his life in a fight with Native people.

1802—The first **sugar mill** is opened on the Hawai'ian islands.

1823—President James Monroe writes the Monroe Doctrine.

1901— James Dole starts the Hawai'ian Pineapple Company in Hawai'i.

1893—The kingdom of Hawai'i is overthrown with the help of the U.S. government.

1825 | **1850** | **1875** | **1900**

1848—Individual ownership of land is allowed for the first time in Hawai'i.

1898—The United States wins the Spanish-American War.

Quiz

ONE
In what year did President James Monroe issue the Monroe Doctrine?

TWO
What British colony was located next to Venezuela in northern South America?

THREE
How many U.S. troops took part in the Spanish-American War?

FOUR
Who were the first people to settle the islands of today's Hawai'i?

FIVE
Who became president of Hawai'i after its queen was removed in 1893?

SIX
When did the Philippines become fully independent?

SEVEN
Who worked on the Spanish sugarcane plantations in Cuba after the Native people had died?

EIGHT
An explosion on which U.S. ship led to the Spanish-American War?

NINE
What were the Native people of Puerto Rico called?

TEN
Who led the Rough Riders?

ANSWERS
ONE 1823 TWO Guiana THREE More than 300,000
FOUR Polynesians FIVE Sanford B. Dole
SIX 1946 SEVEN Slaves from Africa
EIGHT U.S.S. *Maine* NINE Arawaks
TEN Theodore Roosevelt

Key Words

citizens: people in a country or area whose rights are protected by law

colonies: areas that are under the control of another country

commonwealth: an area that is controlled by the United States but is largely able to govern itself

empire: a group of countries or areas under the control of one leader or one country

immunity: the ability to fight off germs and not get sick

international tribunal: a court that settles problems between countries

irrigation: the supplying of water to farm fields by means of a system of pipes, ditches, or streams

missionaries: religious people who travel to an area in order to try to change the religion of other people

plantation: a large farm that grows one or a few crops to be sold

sugar mill: a factory used to produce sugar from sugarcane

taro: a plant that has roots, similar to potatoes, that are good to eat

territory: an area that belongs to or is under the control of a government

trade routes: the routes used for shipping items between two areas that trade, or exchange goods, with each other

Index

LIGHTBOX

SUPPLEMENTARY RESOURCES

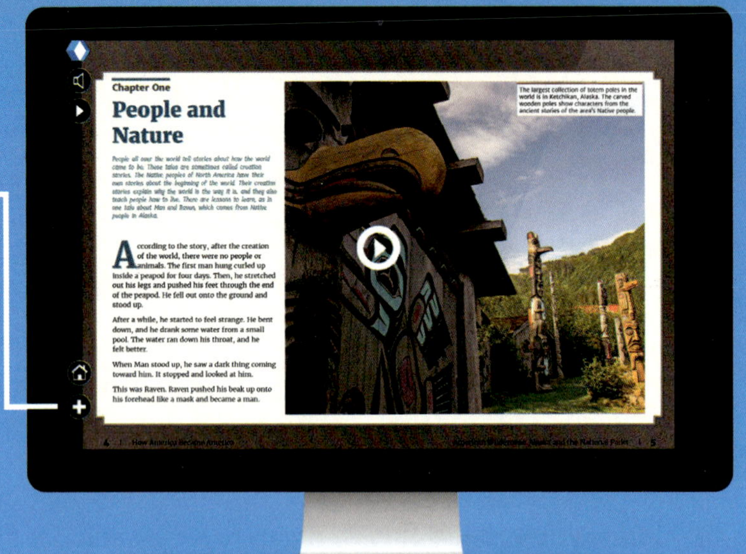

Click on the plus icon found in the bottom left corner of each spread to open additional teacher resources.

- Download and print the book's quizzes and activities
- Access curriculum correlations
- Explore additional web applications that enhance the Lightbox experience

LIGHTBOX DIGITAL TITLES
Packed full of integrated media

VIDEOS

INTERACTIVE MAPS

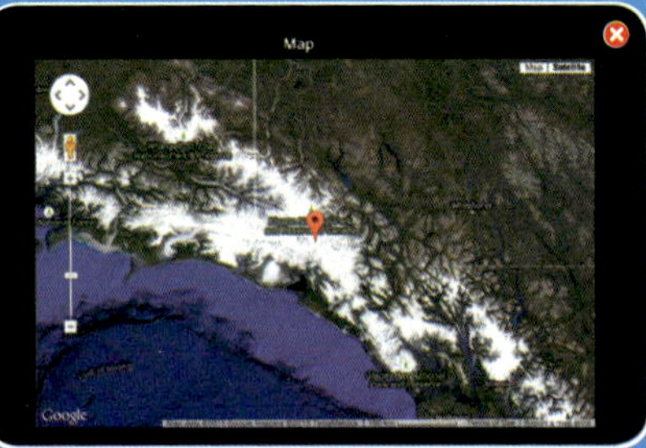

WEBLINKS

SLIDESHOWS

QUIZZES

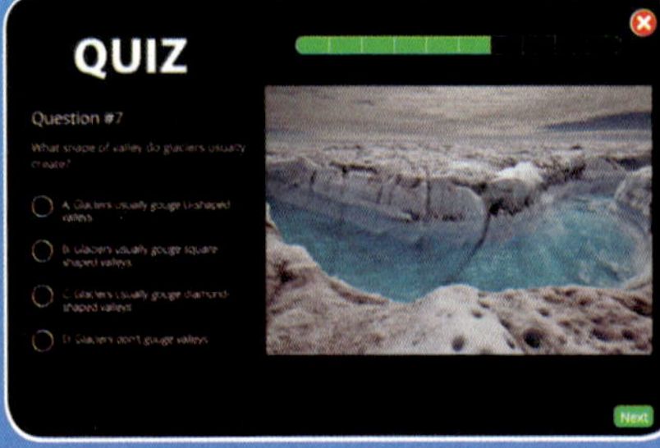

OPTIMIZED FOR

- ✔ TABLETS
- ✔ WHITEBOARDS
- ✔ COMPUTERS
- ✔ AND MUCH MORE!

Published by Smartbook Media Inc.
350 5th Avenue, 59th Floor
New York, NY 10118
Website: www.openlightbox.com

Published by Mason Crest in 2013

062018
121117

Library of Congress Cataloging-in-Publication Data
Names: Sharp, Constance, author.
Title: Beyond our shores (1890/1899) / Constance Sharp.
Other titles: Beyond our shores.
Description: New York, NY : Smartbook Media Inc., [2019] | Series: How America became America | Includes index. | Audience: Grades 4-6. | Identifiers: LCCN 2017054969 (print) | LCCN 2018005552 (ebook) | ISBN 9781510536074 (Multi User ebook) | ISBN 9781510536067 (hardcover : alk. paper)
Subjects: LCSH: United States--Territorial expansion--History--19th century--Juvenile literature. | United States--Foreign relations--1865-1898--Juvenile literature.
Classification: LCC E713 (ebook) | LCC E713 .S525 2019 (print) | DDC 973.8--dc23
LC record available at https://lccn.loc.gov/2017054969

Printed in Brainerd, Minnesota, United States
1 2 3 4 5 6 7 8 9 0 21 20 19 18 17

Project Coordinator Heather Kissock
Art Director Terry Paulhus

Photo Credits
Every reasonable effort has been made to trace ownership and to obtain permission to reprint copyright material. The publisher would be pleased to have any errors or omissions brought to its attention so that they may be corrected in subsequent printings.

The publisher acknowledges Getty Images, Alamy, Dreamstime, Shutterstock, and iStock as its primary image suppliers for this title.